595.4   Martin, Louise
Ma
          Tarantulas

GUMDROP BOOKS - Bethany, Missouri

TARANTULAS

THE SPIDER DISCOVERY LIBRARY

Louise Martin

Rourke Enterprises, Inc.
Vero Beach, Florida 32964

LIBRARY OF CONGRESS
Library of Congress Cataloging-in-Publication Data

Martin, Louise, 1955-
  Tarantulas/by Louise Martin.

    p. cm. — (The Spider discovery library)
  Includes index.
  Summary: Describes characteristics, habits, and natural
environment of the large hairy spiders whose bite is not as
deadly as was once believed.
  ISBN 0-86592-967-X
  1. Tarantulas — Juvenile literature. [1. Tarantulas.
2. Spiders.] I. Title. II. Series: Martin, Louise, 1955-
Spider discovery library.
QL458.42.T5M37   1988   88-5975
595.4'4 - dc19   CIP
                               AC

*Title page photo: Tarantulas like this
can be found in Arizona*

TABLE OF CONTENTS

TARANTULAS

The true tarantulas are the wolf spiders of Europe, which belong to the *Lycosidae* family. They get their name from the city of Taranto in Italy. Tarantulas' bites were believed to cause great sadness in their victims. People called this sadness **"tarentism"** and thought the only way to cure this deathly disease was to do a wild dance, the **tarantella**.

A female wolf spider with her young

TARANTULAS AND PEOPLE

In fact, the bite of the tarantula is not harmful to man. A tarantula bite may be a little painful, but it will not hurt for long. It is certainly not as deadly as was once thought. Scientists have used tarantulas' **venom** in experiments on insects and animals. They found that insects die quickly, but the venom takes up to three days to kill a bird or small animal.

These European tarantulas are not very poisonous

HOW THEY LOOK

The tarantulas we talk of are completely different from the wolf spiders of Europe. They are huge and hairy spiders with large bodies and strong legs. These so-called tarantulas are members of the *Theraphosidae* family, usually grouped under the name of *Mygalomorph* spiders. The *Mygalomorphs*. include bird-eating spiders, funnel web spiders, and trapdoor spiders, as well as the hairy North American tarantulas.

A hairy North American tarantula

HOW THEY GROW

North American male tarantulas live for about ten years. It is believed that females can live as long as twenty-five years. As the spiders grow, they outgrow their skins. Each time they get too big for their skins they shed them, or **molt**. Male tarantulas molt fifteen times before reaching adult size. Until the spiders are fully grown it is impossible to tell whether they are male or female.

Tarantulas can grow very big

Mexican red-knee tarantulas are often kept as pets

A tarantula eats a katydid

WHERE THEY LIVE

North American tarantulas are common in the United States, Mexico, and Central and South American. They are not dangerous to man. If handled roughly, these spiders may give a fairly painful bite, but they are safe enough to keep as pets. One kind of Mexican tarantula with red spots on the legs is often kept as a pet. This has led to a reduction of its numbers in the wild. Tarantulas live in burrows under the ground. They spend most of their lives in their burrows, leaving only at night to hunt for food.

Tarantulas suck their prey dry

WHAT THEY EAT

Tarantulas are **nocturnal** hunters. Each night they leave their burrows in search of food. Tarantulas mostly eat insects found in the area close to their burrow. Giant **species** found in the jungles of South America like to eat small animals, such as frogs, lizards, and snakes. Scientists have found that these large South American tarantulas prefer to eat animals when in captivity.

Tarantulas are normally safe to handle

HOW THEY EAT

Even the largest spiders cannot eat their **prey** whole. They have no way of chewing, so they can only take liquid food. To eat small animals, tarantulas first inject them with venom through their hollow fangs. This **paralyzes** the prey. The large tarantulas then crush the animals, beginning at the head, and use their mouthpieces to suck their juices. It may take a whole day for the tarantulas to eat their prey in this way.

A tarantula in the defensive posture

PREDATORS

The tarantulas' underground burrows hide them from many possible **predators**. The spiders' most dangerous enemies are spider-hunting wasps. In North America these wasps are often called "tarantula hawks" because they prey heavily on tarantulas. Often the tarantulas rush out of their burrows thinking the wasps are prey, and are attacked by them instead. Sometimes, the wasps enter the burrows to attack the spiders.

A spider-hunting wasp drags off prey

THEIR DEFENSES

The attacking wasp must be very careful of the tarantula's fangs. The wasp must strike first with its sting. The first sting may be in the tarantula's head, paralyzing the spider's fangs. The second sting, in the spider's underside, paralyzes the whole spider. Once the tarantula can no longer move, the wasp drags it off to become food for its young.

Glossary

to molt (MOLT) — to shed an outer layer of skin or hair

nocturnal (noc TUR nal) — active at night

paralyze (PAR a lyze) — to make a person or animal unable to move

predator (PRED a tor) — an animal that hunts others for food

prey (PREY) — an animal that is hunted for food

species (SPE cies) — a scientific term meaning type or kind

tarantella (tar an TELL a) — a wild dance believed to cure victims of tarantula bites

tarentism (TAR ent ism) — a disease that makes people very sad

venom (VEN om) — poison

INDEX